# SNOT BUBBLES!

*For the ladies in the stands...*

To Jerrod and Kirsten
You are the lights of my life. May responsibility as well as happiness always sit comfortably on your shoulders. Remember, challenge is good. Don't forget to enjoy the game.

And to Jerry
Thanks for challenging me to challenge myself, for remaining even when the game gets tough, and most of all, for being one heck of a great team mate.

## ACKNOWLEDGMENTS

Special thanks to a prince among men and the greatest of editors, Fred Warren of Woodward Academy.

# SNOT BUBBLES!

# A Football Primer for Moms, Wives and Significant Others

Helma Clark

**Illustrated by: David Goodrich**

Caricatures: Kirsten Clark
Computer Graphics: Jerrod Clark

JERSTEN PRESS

PRINTING HISTORY
First Edition          October 2000

ISBN:  0-9702793-0-2

JERSTEN PRESS
P.O. Box 688, McDonough, GA 30253-0688
Phone (770)474-7545 * Fax (770)474-7545
Helmaclark@aol.com

***Quantity Buyers***
Discounts on this book are available for bulk
purchases.
Write or call for information on our discount
program.

# TABLE OF CONTENTS

# INTRODUCTION

"Snot Bubbles" is a term used to describe the situation in which a football player (usually a lineman) hits a player from the opposing team so hard that snot bubbles literally emit from the downed player. It is one step down from "ten toed" where the opposing player is hit with such force that he lands flat on his back, ten toes up, presumably unconscious.

"Snot Bubbles" also occur when we moms, wives and significant others sit in the stands in the fall and winter on cold bums, with love in our hearts, laryngitis and our own snot bubbles (because our faces are frozen numb and we don't feel the drainage), and cheer our guys on.

It's all part of the game of football, a game that, for the most part has been a male played and male appreciated sport.

Not any more. Today, more and more women are, for one reason or another, tuning in and turning on to football. What once was regarded as a bunch of grunting, sweating Neanderthals, is being looked upon by the women of today as a group of well orchestrated warriors. Not only are they fighting machines, they are current day knights in a strategically maneuvered chess match.

And if they are our sons, they are the most important boys in the world, with some crazy need to be pummeled by all sorts of monsters.

Three years ago my son announced that he was going to play seventh grade football. His parents' initial response was a resounding and unified, "I don't think so."

The next day he went out for the team. And much to my maternal chagrin, there were no cuts in 7th grade football. So for eight weeks, every weekday afternoon, I planted my daughter and myself on the Woodward Academy practice field bleachers and waited for my darling baby boy to get crushed.

In those eight weeks we watched a team of young adolescent boys hike, hit, scramble, tackle, and run until they puked. Some quit, but no one got crushed.

It's not easy watching your child undergo physical and mental assault on a daily basis. It's frustrating when he jumps into the car after practice, hooting about his "sack," and you haven't a clue what he's talking about. And it is downright depressing when he has to wait while your ten-year-old daughter explains it to you.

Thus, the study began.

What you are about to read is a three year educational process...condensed. This book is not intended to be comprehensive. It is a *primer*, one that can be easily carried in your purse or pocket. And although all are welcome to read it, it is aimed primarily at women...women without a clue- the football widow tired of feeling like a foreigner in her own home on Monday night, the significant other seeking knowledge and more commonality with a guy she considers worth the effort.

*Snot Bubbles* is also written for women like me, moms of football players who want to share and understand what is certain to be some very significant moments in their young sons' lives. For although it is reward enough to drive them around and feed them huge amounts of food, it is a rush to spot an "off sides" before the flag comes out.

To aid in the instruction, the chapters are divided into the basics of the game, sub-titled with cheers most of us have heard at one time or another. Although I have inserted a fair amount of editorial, the basic information is, to the best of my research ability, accurate. When you finish *Snot Bubbles*, you should have a *beginning* knowledge of the fascinating and exciting game of football, a game in which the learning, like the excitement, never ends.

Keeping that in mind, I have recommended books in

Chapter 8 to further extend your education. There is however, no substitute for going to the games and practices and asking questions. I have yet to meet a football lover who is not more than happy to explain the sport in detail.

# CHAPTER 1

*"We want a touchdown! What's that? Six points!"*

## THE OBJECT OF THE GAME

"[Football] is the language of men."

Leslie Vissar, a female sports' commentator, is credited with that statement. And it couldn't be truer. Because football games, like men themselves, are based on acquisition and protection of territory.

The typical woman will fight over many things, but rarely will she raise her pressure over a few inches of turf. But, as witnessed by the 2000 Superbowl, that is exactly what men...big men, well paid men, seemingly otherwise intelligent men...will bleed, sweat and risk their bodies for. It is, as they say, the object of the game.

At the base of any given football game, there is only one goal: Invade the other guys' territory. When you look down at that great, big football field (100 yards to be exact), you will see a set of upright poles at each end. Those are **goal posts**. The line in front each goal post is called the **goal line**.

That mass of grunting, sweating males on the field is really two teams. And they each want to invade the others' goal line while carrying the ball. Exactly how they accomplish this is covered later. But once they do it, they have earned a **touchdown.**

The closest analogy I can come up with is a Macy's One Day Sale. Think cashmere. Think 90% off. And you and the woman across the table have both spotted the last medium turtleneck...in oatmeal.

Imagine the sweater to be the football. And the cash register is the goal line. That's the simplistic object of the game.

Football, however, is far from simple. It is, to use another analogy, a chess match of sorts. More accurately, every play in the game is a chess match. At the beginning of each play, the players must be in their assigned positions. The moves each makes once play commences is determined by the position he plays.

The objective of each player on any given play may be different, but the team objective is the same: Get points by moving the ball down the field toward and across the opposing team's goal line and prevent the opponent from doing the same. The choreography and execution that accomplishes this goal can either be a masterpiece or a disaster.

## JUST THE FACTS

1. The football field is 100 yards long.

2. At each end of the field is an **end zone**, where **touch-downs** occur.

3. When a team successfully moves the ball down the field and into the end zone, it gets a touchdown. Six points.

4. After the touchdown is made, the team who has just made the touchdown can either go for the **extra point** or attempt a **conversion.**

    a. An **extra point** is made when the team who just made the touchdown takes the ball back out to the three yard line and successfully kicks the ball between the uprights of the goal post, for one additional point (See diagram on page 15).

    b. A **conversion** is when, after the touchdown, the team takes the ball on the three yard line and moves it into the end zone...again, for two additional points.

5. Two other ways to get points are with a **field goal** and a **safety.** Both of these will be discussed in depth later on. But for now:

a.  A **field goal** attempt is like an extra point, except that it is attempted from farther out on the field, usually on a fourth down.  It is worth 3 points.

b. A **safety** occurs when the team that has possession of the ball is tackled in its own end zone. (In other words, 100 yards from where he wants to go.)  It is worth 2 points to the team who made the tackle.

Now that you know the object of the game, lets get down and dirty.  Really dirty.

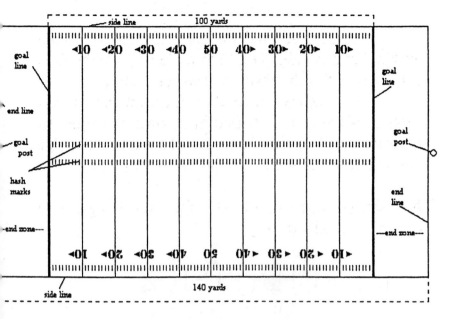

## The Football Field

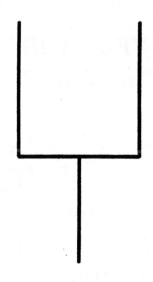

## Goal Post

# CHAPTER 2

*"We Are the Eagles, the Mighty, Mighty Eagles..."*

## THE PLAYERS AND THEIR POSITIONS

On any given play, there are twenty-two players on the field, eleven on each team. The eleven players who have possession of the ball are called **the offense.** Their job is to score. The job of the **defense** is to prevent the offense from scoring.

You can usually determine the position a player is playing by noting where they are in relation to the **line of scrimmage** before the play commences. The line of scrimmage is the imaginary line upon which the ball is placed at the beginning of each play. The players line up according to this line. So if the ball is placed on the ten yard line, that is the line of scrimmage. The offense must line up behind this line, and the defense in front of it.

As you read through the player's positions and responsibilities, be sure and look at the diagram on pages 28 and 29 so you can visualize them on the field. That way their jobs make more sense.

# OFFENSE

The players on offense fill the following positions:

## OFFENSIVE LINEMEN

(There are five.) These are the guys in a line in front of the quarterback (just behind the line of scrimmage). They are usually big (huge when you see them up close), and strong. It helps if they are mean.

The job of the linemen is to protect the quarterback and the ball carrier. They also physically create "lanes" for the ball carrier to run through or for the man throwing the ball to throw through.

To get an idea of their job, imagine war. These are the guys on the front line. All that grunting and carrying on you hear right after the ball is snapped (hiked) is usually created by the linemen.

There are three types of offensive linemen. The **Center**

who **snaps** or hikes the ball between his legs to the quarterback. As soon as he finishes that delicate action- which, if done wrong can cause all kinds of chaos- he blocks the opposing linemen.

The two **Guards** line up next to the center. And the two **Tackles** line up outside each guard.

## QUARTERBACK

(There is one.) The **quarterback** is the man who controls the play. He will take the snap (hike), then either throw (or pass) the ball to one of the **receivers** or he will hand the ball off, literally, to one of the **running backs.**

Quarterbacks can also **run** the ball, which means once they get the ball, they run with it themselves. Since they are typically of smaller stature than a lineman, this is a big risk, because the linemen on defense are made like offensive linemen. Think deer (quarterback) and bull (defensive lineman).

The quarterback is the center of attention, both inside and outside the game. Chances are you've come across at least one NFL quarterback in a commercial. San Francisco's Steve Young comes to mind. He is seen in pain reliever advertisements, probably because of his tendency to run the ball a lot.

An important trait in quarterbacking is the ability to bind the team. A quarterback whose ego is larger than his entire line is a detriment to the team. Why? Because of his position.

The quarterback manages the plays. Even if the coach orders a particular play from the sidelines (i.e. pass to a wide receiver), once the ball is snapped, the quarterback is the person who has to adapt to the defense and make changes on a moment's notice. That means he must be intelligent enough to know all the plays, all the players, their strengths and weaknesses, and within a split second, be able to assess the opposing teams' defense.

He is also dependent upon his fellow players to: a) keep the defensive line from eating him alive, and b) get into position on the field so he can deliver the ball.

So it's easy to see how important it is for this player to not only have a great throwing arm, but also a talent for inspiring his team mates.

If the quarterback has spent his time in practice tearing down his team mates and boasting of his own superiority, he has, by game time, lost the trust and respect of his comrades and protectors. Not wise.

I was privy to a hassling session from a quarterback once. It was right before one of my son's eighth grade games. I had gotten there early and overheard the quarterback of the opposing team blast his linemen for a good ten minutes before they went on the field for warm ups.

"You guys s———, you know that? I work my a— to make the plays, and you pu———s can't even block. You're worthless. Now, I mean it. You had better block today. If I get hurt, it'll be your a———es...."

No one spoke in response. Since my son was playing offensive line at the time, I had a strong urge to tell the quarterback a thing or two myself, even if he was on the opposing team. (Of course, my second response was to wash the boy's mouth out with soap.)

Just before the game started, I mentioned the episode to one of the dads who happened to have played the game in high school.

He laughed. "Get ready to celebrate," he announced. "Our boys are about to have a major ego boost."

My confusion didn't last long. On the first play of the game, the opposing team had possession of the ball. As soon as the ball was snapped, the offensive line opened up like Moses' parting of the sea. Our boys were all over that quarterback. The entire game went that way, until they finally took the poor kid out.

I've wondered many times if he ever realized what had happened.


## WIDE RECEIVERS

(There are two.) These are the guys who usually catch the ball when the quarterback throws it. They are fast...real fast.

Before the snap, they are usually lined up distantly to the right or left of the linemen.

Barnes & Noble Booksellers
18300 NW Evergreen Parkway
Beaverton, OR 97006
(503) 645-3046
11-21-01 S02748 R005

Snot Bubbles: A Football          8.95N
0970279302

SUB TOTAL                         8.95
TOTAL                             8.95
AMOUNT TENDERED
CASH                             10.00


TOTAL PAYMENT                    10.00
CHANGE
        Thank you for Shopping at
        Barnes & Noble Booksellers
Shop online 24 hours a day www.bn.com
#96347  11-21-01 04:15P DAN S


        Booksellers Since 1873

Full refund issued for new and unread books and unopened music withi
days with a receipt from any Barnes & Noble store.
Store Credit issued for new and unread books and unopened music afte
days or without a sales receipt. Credit issued at <u>lowest sale price</u>.
We gladly accept returns of new and unread books and unopened music f
bn.com with a bn.com receipt for store credit at the bn.com price.

Full refund issued for new and unread books and unopened music withi
days with a receipt from any Barnes & Noble store.
Store Credit issued for new and unread books and unopened music afte
days or without a sales receipt. Credit issued at <u>lowest sale price</u>.
We gladly accept returns of new and unread books and unopened music f
bn.com with a bn.com receipt for store credit at the bn.com price.

**Wide receivers** are also high profile players. They have to get down the field in a hurry, then catch long passes while being pursued by the defense. Thus, they are at the center of big, beautiful exciting plays.

If the play is a "running play," wide receivers will act as blockers so the running backs can get through.

There are two types of wide receivers. **Split ends** line up on the line of scrimmage on the side away from the tight end (see below). The other wide receiver, the **Flanker,** usually lines up on the same side as the tight end and one yard behind the line of scrimmage.

We'll talk about the importance of the position of these players more when we discuss offensive formations.

## RUNNING BACKS

(There are two.) When you're watching a game and the ball just seems to disappear from the quarterback's hands, he's probably handed off the ball to a **running back.**

These guys usually line up behind the quarterback before the snap. After the ball is hiked, the quarterback hands the ball to the running back (on a **rushing,** or running play). The running back's job is to move through the "lanes" that the offensive linemen have, hopefully, provided.

There are two running backs. The **fullback** usually leads

the **halfback** on running plays. He will be the lead blocker on such plays. For this reason, fullbacks are usually really big and not extremely graceful.

Running Backs can also catch passes.

**Halfbacks** are usually smaller than fullbacks, but not much. Typically, halfbacks depend on the fullback to create the hole he needs to get through with the ball.

## TIGHT ENDS

(Yes, most of the players have them, but there is usually only one player on the field at a time with the title.) **Tight ends** are either receivers or linemen, depending upon the play.

In a running play, they block like linemen. They also catch passes.

Before the snap, you'll find the tight end lined up next to the offensive tackle behind the line of scrimmage.

# DEFENSE

The players on defense fill the following positions:

## DEFENSIVE LINEMEN

(There are usually four.) These guys are made like offensive linemen. They have to be big because the "trench warfare" that takes place on the field is between these two sets of players.

They line up right across the line of scrimmage from the offensive linemen. There are usually two **tackles**, located in the middle of the defensive line and two **ends**, one outside each tackle.

**Defensive linemen** are responsible for stopping the runner (i.e. the running back in the event of a running play) and attacking the quarterback, hopefully **sacking**, or tackling him before he can pass the ball.

## LINEBACKERS

(There are usually four.) These are the guys lined up a few yards behind the defensive linemen. As you can imagine from their location on the field, they have to be more agile and faster than the linemen.

**Linebackers** have many jobs. They must stop a ball carrier if he gets past the defensive line. They **rush**, or attempt to get to the quarterback. And they must be ready to defend against passes to the receivers.

It is said that linebackers are the most athletic players on the field. When you consider all they have to do, you can understand why.

## CORNERBACKS

(There are two.) The **cornerbacks'** job is to cover the receivers. Remember that I said the receivers are fast. Well, the cornerbacks have to not only keep up with them, their job is to **intercept,** or catch the passes intended for the receivers. At the very least they must keep the receivers from catching the pass... without touching them before the ball is in their hands. (Interference will be covered in the chapter on penalties.)

In the event a pass is not thrown, the cornerbacks are responsible for tackling the ball carrier.

## SAFETIES

(There are two.) As distinguished from the particular play of the same name which I have already discussed, **safety** is also a position on defense.

Safeties are usually smaller... and they can run. They are the safety net, or the last line of defense against the ball carrier. By the time the man carrying the ball has gotten past the defensive linemen and the linebackers, he's looking at the open field and cooking with gas. The safety is the only one left to stop him. He has to catch him first, though. Thus, speed is imperative.

There are two types of safeties, the **strong safety** and the **free safety.** The names are dependent upon their position on the field. The strong safety plays behind the linebackers, on the same side of the field as the tight end. His role is to cover the tight end and the running back and to prevent a run past the line.

The free safety is positioned in the middle of the field past the middle linebacker and directly opposite the center and quarterback. He is the furthest position on defense. His job is to stop the long run. He can go from sideline to sideline to accomplish his goal.

The free safety must keep all receivers in front of him. He has to be able to catch the receiver in the case of a long run.

And being fast isn't enough. Safeties have to be tough. He has to be willing to attack a large ball carrier who has gained a lot of momentum moving down the field. That takes guts, and there's no easy way to do it.

I heard a player once describe a good safety as a little, fast guy whose Mama never shouted, "Be careful."

******************

## JUST THE FACTS

**OFFENSE**

1.  Offensive Linemen
    a.  Center (1):  Snaps (hikes) the ball, then blocks
    b.  Guards (2): Blocks
    c.  Tackles (2): Blocks

2.	Quarterback (1):  Controls the play by passing, handing off or running

3.	Wide Receivers (2): Catch (receive) the ball when the QB passes; otherwise block
	a.	Split end
	b.	Flanker

4.	Running Backs (2): Takes the ball from the QB on running plays; otherwise blocks
	a.	Fullback
	b.	Halfback

5.	Tight End (1):  Act as both receivers and linemen, depending upon the play.


**DEFENSE**

1.	Defensive Linemen
	a. Tackles (2):  Stop runner and attack quarterback
	b. Ends (2):  Stop runner and attack quarterback

2.	Linebackers (4): Stop the runner, attack the quarterback and defend against passes to receivers

3.	Cornerbacks (2):  Cover the receivers and prevent runs past the line of scrimmage.

4.     Safeties (2): Safety net.
       a.     Strong Safety: Cover the tight end and running back and prevent run past the line of scrimmage
       b.     Free Safety: Stop the long run

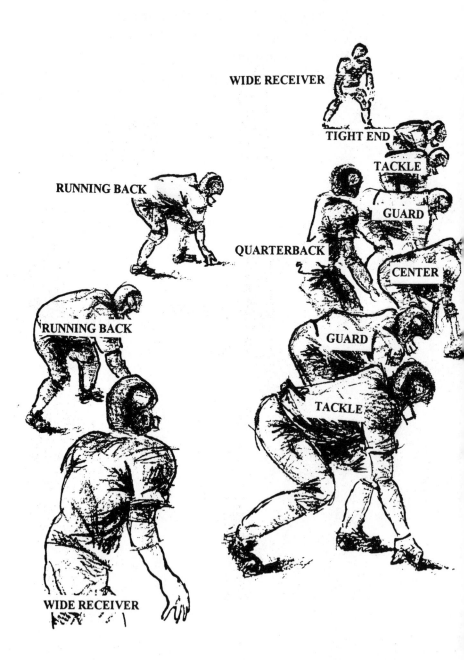

**OFFENSE**

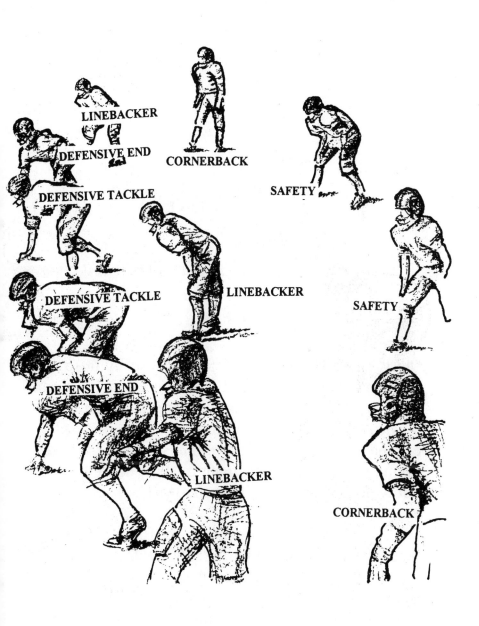

**DEFENSE**

# CHAPTER 3

*"First and Ten! Do It Again! Do It Again!"*

## OFFENSE

Most female novice football fans are usually frustrated by what they see on the field. Even once they figure out that there are two teams down there trying to make touchdowns, and they gain a basic understanding of the players and their positions, one refrain seems to find itself rolling from every female mouth: "Why don't they just throw the ball and make a touchdown?"

Well, Ladies, it's easier said than done. Big passing plays, when successful, are beautiful. They hide the grunting, sweating, backbreaking chaos that's going on at the line and focus on the captivating spiral throw to a living, breathing, sexy package of fluid male muscle. A perfectly orchestrated long pass can take a woman's breath away, literally make her light headed.

But that same attempt can be disastrous by a mere mis-step on the part of any one player. The worst thing that can happen on an offensive play is an **interception.** That's when a defensive player steals the ball from the offense. Major disaster.

Interceptions are much more common on passing plays than they are on running plays. If you think about it, the reason is obvious. There is much more room for mis-take on a passing play, both in yardage and movement.

At this point it is important to understand a major rule in football: As long as the offense can gain ten yards within four **downs**, they get to keep possession of the football. Each play, each time the ball is hiked, is considered a down.

Think of downs as turns. The offense gets four turns to gain ten yards. Once they get those ten yards, it goes back to a first down. Thus, the cheer, *"First and ten. Do it again, do it again!"*

So, all the offense needs to do is get ten yards, every four turns, or 2.5 yards per turn...all the way down the field. And it is important to do this without **turnovers.** A turnover is when the offense loses the ball to the other team either by losing a **fumble** (a dropped ball) or throw-ing an interception. That's why the running play is used more often in football. It just makes sense.

Of course, once you get a close-up look at the men on the defensive line, you begin to understand why getting ten yards in four downs is a big deal. Big enough to cheer about. Those human walls don't let much stuff get past them.

And it's important to understand that the offensive linemen, as opposed to the defensive linemen, cannot "tackle."

There is the story of the mother whose young son was an offensive lineman. The muddy, sweaty boy jumped in the car after a particularly painful loss to another team and asked his adoring mom, "Well, what'd ya think?"

"You're a tackle, right?" the mother clarified.

"Um hmm. And a good one, too. Don't you think?"

"Well, Honey." The mother searched for a way to be positive as she pulled the car out of the school parking lot. "You look real good to me, of course. But maybe if you actually *tackled* someone...."

The boy let out an exasperated sigh. "Mom, I'm offensive."

"Oh, no! I wouldn't say you're offensive. You just need to start tackling those other boys."

What the mother didn't understand was that although her son's position on the field is "tackle," he could only block the guys on the other team, which makes it a lot harder to keep those big guys on defense at bay.

So the idea is to mix it up, keep the defense guessing. Use strategy.

Football games are won and lost on strategy. On any given play, *the offense is required to have seven linemen on the line of scrimmage.* Five of those linemen must be ineligible to catch passes (see Chapter on Penalties for more on this). Other than that, the offense has all sorts of options as to how to position and utilize their players. The positioning of players for different strategic plays is called **formation.** And there are all kinds of formations in football. Here are a few.

# THE SPLIT "T" FORMATION

In this formation both the half back and the full back are in position behind the quarterback off to the side, or "split." Neither is directly behind the quarterback.

The next time you watch a football game, look at the offensive formation. Keeping in mind that, generally, the speed is in the back of the formation and the brawn is in the front, you can begin to figure out what the offense is probably going to do with the ball.

The Split "T" is usually used as a passing formation. But because the offense is "balanced" (i.e. running backs on each side of the quarterback), it is also effective on running plays. The ball can be passed or run equally on both sides of the field.

```
                                                    los
                                                     V
O                    O    O    X    O O    O
SE                             O              TE       O
                              QB                      FL


             O                      O
            HB                     FB



                    Split "T" Formation
```

# THE "I" FORMATION

In this formation, the quarterback is behind the center and the two running backs are in line behind the quarterback. As you can see from the diagram, the formation actually looks like an "I."

```
                                                    los
                                                     V
O                    O    O    X    O O    O
SE                             O              TE
                              QB                      O
                                                     FL

                               O
                              FB
                               O
                              HB
                    "I" Formation
```

# THE OFFSET "I" FORMATION

In this formation, the fullback is "offset" or off to one side a little, while the halfback is still in line behind the quarterback.

```
                                              los
                                               V
O             O   O   X   O O   O
SE                    O           TE       O
                      QB                   FL

         O
         FB
                  O
                  HB
```

**Offset "I" Formation**

# DOUBLE WING "T", OR "ACE" FORMATION (A FAVORITE OF WOODWARD ACADEMY)

In the Ace formation, the line consists of the center, two tackles, two guards, and *two tight ends*. There are two flankers just behind the line and only one running back in the backfield. As you can see, this puts a great deal of power up front, close to the offensive line. This is a great running formation.

```
                                              los
                                               V
_____
           O   O   O   X   O   O   O
           TE          O          TE          O
    O                  QB                      FL
    FL.


                       O
                       R
```

**Double Wing "T" or Ace Formation**

# THE SWEEP

The first time I saw this play, it broke my heart. Our team was playing Westminster, a school in Atlanta whose seventh grade football team looked like an army in 1998. It was the second quarter and we were holding them...somewhat. Westminster had possession of the ball.

As soon as the ball was snapped, it disappeared for a full three seconds. Before our guys could respond, their half back "swept" (parallel to the line of scrimmage) to the far left side of the field, then took off upfield for a touchdown.

They did that four more times to us that day. I later read that this was Vince Lombardi's (Green Bay Packers coach) "weapon" in the 1960's.

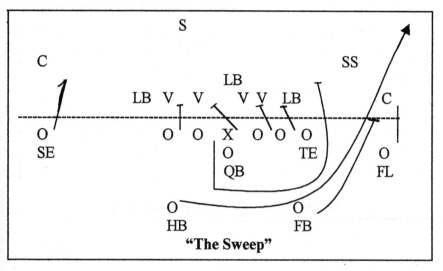

"The Sweep"

# THE SHOTGUN FORMATION

The name of this formation has nothing to do with the position of the receivers. When the quarterback lines up five yards behind the center and receives the snap in the air, it is called a shotgun formation.

The purpose of this formation is to allow the quarterback to get a good look at the field. Thus, it is usually used as a passing formation. Being situated five yards back also saves the quarterback from having to run back after the snap.

# THERE ARE LITERALLY HUNDREDS MORE!

These are just a few of the plays to give you an idea of how the offense can manipulate the two basic rules of seven men on the line and two eligible receivers on the line.

Once you begin watching the game, you'll see all sorts of configurations. The important thing to note is where the power is. Is it mostly on the line like the Double Wing "T" or is there a lot in the backfield like the Split "T"?

The best teams are able to mix it up, always changing formations ...always keeping the defense guessing.

# JUST THE FACTS

1.    The offense gets four **downs** or turns to carry the ball ten yards. If they accomplish  this, they can keep possession of the ball, and it again becomes "first and ten," or first down, ten yards to go.

2.    A **turnover** means the opposing team gets the ball from the offense either because the offense threw an **interception** (the quarterback threw the ball and a player from the opposing team caught it) or the opposing team recovers a **fumble** (when an offensive player in possession of the ball drops it).

3.   A possession change occurs when the offense can't gain ten yards of territory within four downs. Then the opposing team takes the ball wherever the last play ended. So if the offense moved the ball to the fifty yard line, that's where the opposition will take up the ball.

4.   Part of the strategy of offense is to keep the defense guessing. To accomplish this, the offense will constantly change **formations** or configurations on the field.

5.   The basic rule of offensive formation is that there must be, on any given play, seven linemen on the line of scrimmage, and five of those linemen must be ineligible to catch passes. (The two men on the outside of the line are eligible receivers.) This leaves a tremendous amount of possibilities for mixing up formations.

# CHAPTER 4

*"Push 'em back! Push 'em back! Wa-a-a-y Back!"*

# DEFENSE

*"Football is a game of defense and field position."*
General Robert Neyland

*"You've got to do everything well, but you've got to play defense first."* Vince Dooley

These are quotes by famous, successful football coaches. The more you are around the game, the more often you will hear the same quotes in so many different words.

The offense has one objective: Get to the end zone. As you have seen, they have numerous ways in which to accomplish that. The defense must stop them, and they have to do it without knowing exactly which play is about to be performed. So they have to think fast and they have to *be* fast.

For the novice football fan to grasp defensive plays, it is easiest to think of the defense as three groups or "waves" of guys. The first wave consists of the **defensive line**. Keeping in mind that these are the biggest guys on the team, it is easy to understand their job: Bust the offensive linemen and create holes. If a lineman happens to get farther along and "sack" a quarterback, then the defense has accomplished its goal in the first wave.

Otherwise, if the linemen do their job well, the second group, the **linebackers**, can move through those holes and get to the ball carrier.

If the ball successfully gets past the first two waves of defense, the third group comes into play, the **secondary** or **defensive backs**. These are the two cornerbacks and two safeties, and their job is to take out a ball carrier who has gotten past the first two groups. They are "the last line of defense" on any given play.

## DEFENSIVE FORMATIONS

In order to keep the ball from getting past the first two waves of the defense, there are basically two formations: 4-3 defense and 3-4 defense. The 3-4 defense places three linemen on the line and four linebackers behind them.

The 4-3 defense means that there are four linemen on the line backed up by three linebackers. This configuration places more pressure on the quarterback because you have more power up front. And it is more effective in stopping the running game.

## DEFENSIVE COVERAGE

In addition, there are two basic types of coverage by the defense: the **zone** and the **man to man**.

In a **zone** defense, the linebackers and defensive backs cover a specific area on the field.

**Man-to-man** defense is where linebackers and defensive backs cover a particular offensive player regardless of where they go on the field. This type of coverage is used when the coaches believe they have enough talent in defensive backs to gamble on each one. In other words, they believe that each of their individual players are equally as fast, agile and strong as the offensive men they cover.

Zone defense is considered a waiting game. The defense basically waits for the offense to make a mistake. Man-to-man defense is more gutsy. It attempts to force the offense to make mistakes.

**Line stunts** are used by the defense to confuse and weaken the offense. In this tactic, two of the defensive linemen will exchange their attack positioning as soon as the ball is snapped. There are many different stunts depending upon who is changing position with whom. But if executed properly, they all have the same effect. Mistakes by the offense.

# DEFENSIVE STRATEGY

Part of the defensive strategy is to control the tempo of the game. Logic would dictate that the offense would control the tempo of the game. They are, after all, the ones who decide how they are going to move the ball down the field.

But a good defense can manipulate the offense. To do this, a defense has to have a great line. If the defensive line can dominate the offensive line, it can effectively force the offense to throw the ball. That means the "meat and potatoes" of a good offense, the running game, is destroyed.

**Blitzing** is one way the defense can control the tempo of the game. A blitz is when more than five defensive players rush at the quarterback as soon as the ball is snapped. This gives the quarterback two choices: 1) throw the ball immediately, or 2) get sacked. Any quarterback with a brain will get rid of the ball.

# DECISION MAKING

By nature, defensive decisions are made in anticipation or reaction to the offense. The best way to watch this decision making in action is to watch the defense right before the ball is snapped. If you're located close to the field, you can hear one of the guys yelling things like "Four wides!" (That means the offense has positioned four wide receivers in preparation for a pass.) Then there will be a scramble of players, seemingly changing position.

Usually one of the linebackers calls what he sees on the offense. Then the defense will rearrange at the last minute in a formation better suited.

If we were able to look into the mind of a defensive player just before the snap, past the adrenaline and the red haze of rage, we would see a systematic analysis of: 1) the offensive formation and what this particular offense usually does with this formation (info gained by film study of the opposing team), 2) their location on the field, 3) where the receivers are located and how many there are, 4) the quarterback's strengths and weaknesses, 5) the receivers' strengths and weaknesses, and hundreds of other pieces of information pertinent to the play at hand. All this information must be observed and analyzed, and all within the few seconds before the ball is hiked.

And here, we thought football was mindless!


## JUST THE FACTS

1.     The job of the defense is to keep the offense from getting a first down, and if possible, to steal the

ball.

2.     In order to accomplish this goal, the defense will use different strategies to:

    a.  Control the tempo of the game,

    b.  Confuse the offense, and/or

    c.  Pressure the quarterback into passing the ball, thereby weakening or removing the offense's running game

3.     There are two basic defensive formations:

    a.  4-3 defense where there are four linemen on the line backed up by three linebackers

    b.  3-4 defense where there are three linemen on the line, backed up by four linebackers

4.     There are two basic types of defensive coverage:

    a.  **Man-to-man**, where each linebacker and defensive back covers a particular offensive player, regardless of where he goes on the field

    b.  **Zone**, where the linebackers and defensive backs cover a specific area on the field

5.     **Line Stunts** are defensive attack position switches just before the snap, used to confuse the offense.

# CHAPTER 5

*"Block That Kick!"*

## SPECIAL TEAMS

**Special Teams** refers to those football players who participate in one of the following plays:
1)The Kickoff
2)The Punt
3)The Field Goal
4)The Extra Point (After Touchdown)

## THE KICKOFF

It is the beginning of the game. The Star Spangled Banner has been sung and tensions are high as the **Kickoff Team** and **Kickoff Return Team** enter the field. The fans stand, many raising their arms in the air and voicing a constant hum.

Out on the field a solitary man sets a football on the center of the thirty yard line, then backsteps. Ten of his team mates fan out on each side of him. As he raises his hand the humming chant gets louder, higher pitched, almost frantic. And when he finally drops his arm, all chaos breaks loose.

That chaos you see on the field is actually highly orchestrated. Every man has a particular responsibility which has been practiced over and over under varying scenarios. It is beyond the scope of this Primer to go into the different jobs and strategies of each of the Special Teams players. But here are the basics of the kickoff.

The kickoff occurs at three different times during the game:

1. The beginning of each game
2. The start of the second half of the game, and
3. Following any scoring play.

**The Kicker**

The Kicker kicks the ball to the Kickoff Return or Receiving Team. He has one job: Kick accurately. Distance kicking is not his only objective. There will be times in the game when the kicker may want to do what is called an **onside kick.**

One rule of the kickoff is that once the ball has travelled at least ten yards, any man on the kickoff team can recover the ball for his team. If a team is behind toward the end of the game and needs possession badly, they may have the kicker (if he is a good kicker) kick the ball in a side direction, starting low, bouncing end over end and taking a high bounce just before it gets ten yards. This **onside kick** allows the kicking team to jump up and, hopefully, retrieve the ball. It is a risky maneuver, one that is only used in desperate times. Because if the receiving team ends up getting the ball, they are that much closer to the goal line.

### The Kick Returner

The guy on the receiving team who catches the ball is called the **Kick Returner**. These guys are usually fast as lightning and tough as nails. It's their job to get the ball and run like the wind, hopefully right past the opposing goal line. He is surrounded by blockers, whose job it is to keep him safe...and running.

The spot where the kick returner ends up getting tackled or taken out of bounds is where the next line of scrimmage will be. So if you were wondering what all the excitement was about with the kickoff, you know now. "It's all about field position."

## THE PUNT

You already know that the offense has four downs or turns to move the ball ten yards. If they don't make it ten yards, then the opposing team takes up the ball on whatever yardline it lays after the fourth down. So if Team A's offense only gets to the nine yard line in four downs, Team B takes up the ball there and heads in the other direction, putting the ball on Team A's 9 yard line for Team B. (See the field diagram on page 15).

As you can see, that would be disastrous for Team A. So, after the third down, if there is a strong chance that they won't get ten yards and they are sitting dangerously close to their own goal line, Team A will choose to **punt**, or kick the ball as far as possible toward Team B's goal line.

On the fourth down, the **punter**, or the guy kicking the ball will line up 15 yards behind the center. The center hikes the ball to the punter, and the punter kicks the ball as far as he can toward the other goal line.

A good punt has two things: distance and **hang time**. Hang time is the time the ball is actually in the air after it has been kicked. The longer the ball stays in the air, the more time the punting team has to get down the field and grab the guy with the ball, the **returner.**

The punting team has to protect the punter so he can make a good punt, then get down the field as fast as possible and tackle the returner.

# THE FIELD GOAL

If, on a fourth down, the team playing offense is close enough to the opposing team's goal post, but doesn't have a very good chance of getting the necessary ten yards, they may decide to kick a **field goal.** In a field goal, the center will hike the ball about seven yards to a ball holder who (very quickly) sets the ball for the kicker. The kicker then kicks the ball through the uprights of the opposing team's goal post.

As discussed in Chapter 1, a successful field goal attempt is worth three points. And many, many games have been won on a field goal. So the defense works hard to thwart the kicker. How? By blocking the kick. Yes, by placing their bodies in front of the ball as it is leaving the ground, straight off the toe of the kicker. So while we ladies are chanting, "Block that kick! Block that kick!" some poor guy takes it seriously and gets every molecule of oxygen knocked right out of him...all for the love of the game.

The defense has to be especially careful when the offense is kicking a field goal. Because it's not past any team to make a fake play. That is, line up in field goal formation, hike the ball, and while the defense is all set up to block the kick, march right in to a first down, or better, to the end zone for a touchdown.

# THE EXTRA POINT

As discussed in the first chapter, there are two ways to score after a touchdown. The team who just made the touchdown can go for a **conversion,** worth two points. Or it can take the higher odds approach of kicking the **extra point**.

The extra point is just what it says, an extra point... only one. To make the extra point, the ball is placed on the three yard line. The center hikes the ball to a ballholder who is kneeling seven yards behind the line of scrimmage.

The ball holder quickly sets the ball with one pointed end down, then holds the other pointed end while the kicker tries to kick the ball through the uprights on the goal post.

If the ball goes through the uprights, the team gets an extra point. So with the touchdown and the extra point, the team has just made seven points.

It is important to note that although the extra point is a given in most high school, college and professional games, if a team doesn't have a good kicker, they are better off going for the more difficult **two point conversion** where the ball is placed at the three yard line and the offense attempts to cross the goal line again.

# JUST THE FACTS

1.     Special Teams consists of players in the following situations:

1)     The Kickoff
2)     The Punt
3)     The Field Goal
4)     The Extra Point

2.     The **kickoff** occurs at the beginning of each game, the start of the second half of the game, and following any scoring play.

3.     When the offense is unable to gain ten yards in three downs,  and they are closer to their own goal line than is comfortable, they may elect to **punt** the ball. This means that on their fourth down, they kick the ball down the field to the opposing team before a possession change.

4.     When the offense is close to the opposition's goal line, but unable to get a first down, they may attempt a **field goal**. The ball is hiked to a ball holder, who places the ball quickly for the kicker. The kicker then attempts to kick the ball through the uprights over the goal post. If successful, a field goal is worth 3 points.

5.     Once a team has made a touchdown, they are allowed to embellish it with **the extra point**. The ball is placed on the three yard line. It is hiked to a ball holder who quickly sets it up for the kicker. The kicker at-

tempts to kick the ball between the uprights over the goal post. If he is successful, the team gets an additional one point.

6.    The extra point is, in theory, easier to accomplish than the two point conversion (where the team who just made the touchdown places the ball on the three yard line and basically attempts to cross the goal line again). That is why a successful conversion is worth the extra point.

# CHAPTER 6

*"Hit 'em a lick. Hit 'em a lick. Harder! Harder!"*

# PENALTIES

Possibly the quickest path to a football education is found by paying attention to the penalties. Because although the rules seem basic, a true football novice is rapidly confused by the nuances of the game.

Therefore, a great deal of space is devoted to this chapter. "Guys on the Side" is a brief discussion of coaches and officials. The basic signals (not penalties) are covered in this area. Then comes the actual penalty signals. The best approach to learning the penalties is to take the book with you to the games and look up the referee signal as it occurs.

# GUYS ON THE SIDE

## THE COACH

Attitude, discipline and basic orchestration of the football game are the responsibilities of the team coach or coaches. Great coaches, make great football teams, make great men. It is fascinating to listen to former football players discuss their coaches. Contrary to the discussion of former teachers, coaches are never described as hard or easy. They are described in terms of character-their own character and the character they instill in their players.

There seems to be a very thick line between a coach who is "tough" and one who is "mean." A former football player will refer to a tough coach as though he were a sort of god, but a mean coach is usually give one line of unrepeatable description before the discussion quickly moves on.

Tommy Protho once said, "The coach is the team, and the team is the coach. You reflect each other." Even with my limited experience as a football mom, I can see the truth in that statement. Technique must be taught, discipline reinforced, but attitude is a contagion. It passes from coaches to players like a virus.

Thus, if a coach is infected with a love of the game, his players will love the game. That love of the game doesn't necessarily appear in the form of sweetness and back pats.

Winning is the objective, but the game is all.

## THE OFFICIALS

To keep the game fair is the job of the **officials**. There are seven (yes seven!) different types of officials in the game of football. College and professional games usually use all seven, while high school, middle school and little leagues use less.

The lead official is the **referee**. For our purposes, he is the most important of the officials merely because he oversees the toss at the first of the game and signals the milestones which occur in a particular game and the infractions which result in penalties.

The following are general signals. They do not reflect penalty producing infractions.

## GENERAL SIGNALS

**Touchdown, Field Goal
Successful Extra Point
Two Point Conversion**

**First Down**

**Safety has been scored.**

**Time Out**

**Penalty Refused,
Incomplete Pass, Missed
Field Goal or Extra
Point
Attempt, Play is over**

**Time In**

# INFRACTION

When you are watching a game and an official throws a **yellow flag,** a rule has been broken that could produce a penalty.  Below are many of those infractions and the assigned penalty.  The applicable referee signals are illustrated on the opposing page.

---

The referee rotates his forearms over and over indicating:
**False Start, Illegal Formation or Kickoff**
PENALTY:  Five yards
A **False start** is when an **Offensive Lineman** gets in his set position on the line, then moves within the full second before the snap.  We had a guy on our defense who was great at coming up and jumping just inside the line, causing the opposing offensive lineman to jump just before the ball was snapped.  The opposing team lost more than fifteen yards in one game because of him.

---

**Crowd Noise:** The penalty is loss of a time out, or a five yard penalty on the defense. Also indicates a
**Dead ball:** The ball is dead after the play has ended.

# REFEREE SIGNAL

**False Start, Illegal Formation or
Kickoff or Safety Kick Out of Bounds**

**Crowd Noise**

# INFRACTION

**Delay of Game or Excessive Time Outs:** A team is only allowed three time outs per half. If they call more than that, they are penalized. They are also only give 45 seconds from the end of one play to begin a new one. If they take more than that time, it is call a delay of game. PENALTY: 5 Yards.

---

**Personal Foul:** This occurs when a player does something either to opposing player or an official. It may be hitting after the whistle or fighting. This signal is often followed with another signal that tells what the infraction is. (See the next three below.) These are major infractions. PENALTY: 15 Yards, sometimes first down.

---

**Roughing the Kicker:** This is self explanatory. You don't rough the kicker. PENALTY: 15 Yards There is a difference between roughing the kicker and **Running into the Kicker**, however. Some say it is a matter of intent. Joe Theisman, the famous Super Bowl winning Quarterback for the Washington Redskins argues that it is a matter of acting ability on the part of the kicker. PENALTY: 5 Yards

# REFEREE SIGNAL

### Delay of Game
### Excessive Time Outs

---

### Personal Foul

---

### Roughing the Kicker

# INFRACTION

**Roughing the Passer:**
PENALTY: 15 Yards

---

**Face Mask:** This is the signal when someone holds onto a face mask. If considered deliberate, the PENALTY is that of a Personal Foul: 15 Yards. If considered **Nondeliberate**, the PENALTY is 5 Yards. I have a real problem with the nondeliberate call. How can you grab something like a face mask without meaning to? And the potential for damage is the same. The first year my son played football, a kid grabbed his mask in practice in an attempt to bring him down. I could just visualize my boy's cervical spine popping. It took all my control and all my daughter's physical force to keep me on the bleachers. I wanted to kill that kid. And I don't like the little goat to this day.

# REFEREE SIGNAL

**Roughing the Passer**

**Face Mask**

# INFRACTION

**Ball has been Illegally Touched, Kicked, or Batted.**
PENALTY: Loss of a down

---

**Illegal Forward Pass:** The Quarterback has to throw the ball from behind the line of scrimmage. If he goes past the line of scrimmage before throwing the ball or if he makes a forward pass to a player and that player makes another forward pass, an illegal forward pass has been committed.
PENALTY: 5 Yards and loss of down

---

**Interference:** If a player pushes, trips or blocks another player while that player is attempting to catch a pass, it is considered interference. Note that both players can attempt to catch the pass, they just can't "interfere" with another player.
PENALTY: Defensive Player Interference: The ball is placed at the site of the infraction as though the pass had been successfully caught. Offensive Player Interference: 15 Yards.

# REFEREE SIGNAL

**Ball Has Been Illegally Touched, Kicked or Batted**

---

**Illegal Forward Pass**

---

**Interference**

# INFRACTION

**Offsides or Encroachment:** There is an imaginary line which crosses the field from sideline to sideline. It's coverage is the length of the ball from tip to tip. This thick line is called the **neutral zone.** The players must line up on each side of this area, on the line of scrimmage. If anyone lines up over the line, or if you see someone jump over it before the ball is snapped, that is Offsides or Encroachment. Keep in mind that a defensive lineman who moves over the line before the ball is snapped is offsides. An offensive lineman need only twitch and he's committed a false start.
PENALTY: 5 Yards

---

**Chop Block or Clipping:** A chop block occurs when an offensive lineman hits a defender at the thigh or lower while another offensive player is blocking him. Clipping is when a player hits an opposing player who is not a ball carrier in the back anywhere from the shoulders to the feet.
PENALTY: 15 Yards

---

**Holding:** When an offensive player wraps his arms around a defensive player, that's holding.
PENALTY: 10 Yards

# REFEREE SIGNAL

## Offsides or Encroachment

## Chop Block or Clipping

## Holding

# INFRACTION

**Ineligible Receiver:** As previously discussed, at least seven offensive players must line up on the line of scrimmage. All the players between the end guys are ineligible to receive passes. So if an offensive lineman heads off downfield without running into a defensive lineman, the penalty flag comes out.

Also the signal for:

**Ineligible Member of the Kicking Team Downfield**
PENALTY: 5 Yards

---

**Intentional Grounding:** If the Quarterback throws a pass that he has no intention of trying to complete ( i.e., he's moved way back behind the line of scrimmage and is being rushed, so instead of taking a yardage loss with a sack, he just throws it over to the side so he can keep field position) this is considered an intentional grounding.

PENALTY: 10 yards

---

**Illegal Use of the Hands:** An offensive player cannot put his hands in a defensive player's face, nor can he push a defensive player from behind. If he does, it's called an illegal use of the hands.

PENALTY: 10 Yards

# REFEREE SIGNAL

**Ineligible Receiver, Ineligible Member of Kicking Team**

**Intentional Grounding**

**Illegal Use of the Hands**

# INFRACTION

**Illegal Substitution or Too Many Men on the Field:**
PENALTY: 5 Yards

---

**Illegal Motion:** This is where it gets technical. Suffice it to say that, for the purposes of this Primer, there are shifts and there are motions. Once the Quarterback yells, "Set," the offensive line has to turn to stone. The other players can "shift" to another position, then get set again. The players have to come to a stop before the play begins. If they don't, it's called "motion." Some players (only one at a time) are allowed to be in motion when the ball is snapped, as long as they aren't in motion toward the line of scrimmage. Otherwise, it's illegal.
PENALTY: 5 Yards

# REFEREE SIGNAL

**Illegal Substitution**

**Illegal Motion**

# INFRACTION

**Illegal Shift**:  When an offensive lineman has assumed the three or four point stance, then lifts his hand up prior to the snap
PENALTY: 5 Yards

---

**Player Disqualified**

---

**Loss of Down:**  As a result of penalties

# REFEREE SIGNAL

**Illegal Shift**

**Player Disqualified**

**Loss of Down**

# INFRACTION

**Unsportsmanlike Conduct**
PENALTY: 15 Yards

---

**Pass Juggled In Bounds, Caught Out of Bounds**:
This is an explanation for when there is an incomplete
pass signal for the above conditions

# REFEREE SIGNAL

**Unsportsmanlike Conduct**

---

**Pass Juggled In Bounds, Caught Out of Bounds**

# CHAPTER 7

# WHEN THE GAME'S OVER: A SPECIAL NOTE TO FOOTBALL MOMS

When it comes to my kids' sports, I am a terrible mom. I take my children's' success or failures personally. I have a tendency to second guess, even when I'm unfamiliar with all the facts. And I'm noted for my post ballgame "critique sessions." That's probably why I've been blessed with advice from a number of other, more seasoned sports parents as well as a couple of saintly coaches on the best way to enjoy as well as inspire my kids.

The following is an encapsulation of that advice. Although I am known to occasionally disregard it (to the detriment of myself and my family), it is still good advice because it is, by nature, intended to help those who are most affected...our children. And I find that when I follow it, I am personally much happier. I share it with you in the same spirit in which it was divulged to me and in some cases, in the same tone in which I heard it the first time (for effect)...

A game, won or lost, is filled with literally hundreds of thrilling moments. On any given football play, there are twenty-two players doing something. Each has his moment, usually moments, to remember, to savor. And savoring great moments is what families are for.

The job of hashing bad moments is the job of the coaches.

If your son carried the ball forty yards and dropped it on the one yard line, he carried the ball forty yards. He knows he dropped the ball. And lest he forget, the coach will surely remind him at the next practice while he's doing suicides. You need to remember the run. You need to remind him of the thrill.

When he sacks the quarterback, but fails to recover the fumble, forget the stupid fumble. HE SACKED A QUARTERBACK!

Above all, if he's a lineman, tell him how well he blocked, how powerful he was. By the time he gets to you, he's spent four quarters tearing down brick walls and having those brick walls tear back. Yes, he left a hole open the size of Montana in the third quarter, the one that the linebacker danced right through to sack your quarterback. But what's one hole compared to all the other moments? He deserves some praise. Give it to him.

And feed him. For heaven's sake, give the boy some food... good food. He's building and repairing tissue. Hot dogs and pizza won't get it. There are tons of books out on basic nutrition. If you're nutritionally impaired, get one. Two major culprits of young athletes are lack of physical conditioning and LACK OF FOOD. If he tells you that all he needs is a hot dog and a coke, and you listen to him, you're more of an adolescent than he is. And you're setting him up for failure, and more importantly, for pain. Use your parental head.

A final note: After talking with numerous men about their experiences as football players, I have come to the conclusion that football teaches life lessons in a magnified form. One of these is the success potential of team cohesiveness. Football players don't have winning seasons, teams do. The entire team wins and the entire team loses.

As a parent, it is your job to reinforce this. The moment you single your child as the only "decent player" on the team, you are not only creating a monster whose chances at success in life are few, but you are helping to destroy an entire team.

Stories abound of teams who start a season with a well-coached, cohesive group of players who perform like a fighting machine, only to end up miserably after a couple of parents decided their sons were too good for every-one else. And not only does the team suffer, the parents who caused the mess ended up marring their own sons' reputations.

If your son is faster, bigger, brighter and stronger than everyone on the team. If he's the only reason his team is winning games, and if he knows more than the coaches do, don't waste him on the trivial. The NFL is always looking for a prodigy.

Otherwise, if your son is a normal, game-loving male, allow him to enjoy the game, for the sake of the game. Let's face it, few of our sons will play in the NFL. And if that is your desire for your child, I recommend the book *The Dark Side of the Game* by Tim Greene.

Hopefully, most of our sons will grow up to be healthy, game-loving men- men who understand challenge and don't mind getting dirty to meet it, men who respect authority but aren't fearful of it; who can take advice, but aren't limited by it.

That is what we wish for our sons.

And so we sit outside in Fall and Winter on cold bums, with love in our hearts, laryngitis and our own snot bubbles (because our faces are frozen numb and we don't feel the drainage), and cheer these future men on.

# CHAPTER 8

# THE EDUCATION CONTINUES

The following are some good books to read now that you have the basics:

1.     *The Complete Idiot's Guide to Understanding Football like a Pro.* This book is written by Joe Theisman with Brian Tarcy. Joe Theisman was the winning quarterback in Superbowl XVII, so he obviously knows just about all there is to know about football.  It is a great book filled  with lots of personality.  It covers just about **all** of NFL football.  Just keep in mind as you're reading that some of the rules for Little Leage, Middle School, etc. are a bit different.

2.     *Football 101, Understanding the Game,* by David R. Walker.  This is probably a good second book to read. It isn't as in depth as the NFL books are, and because he

has played and coached at the different levels of football, Walker covers the rules at different levels. I've got to admit that, as a mom, my favorite part of this book is its Foreword written by Steve Young. He talks about some of his Little League experiences and the life lessons that football has taught him. Most importantly, Young covers the most important rule for us moms: "Mothers do not come out on the field!"

3. *Football for Dummies* by Howie Long with John Czarnecki is similar to *The Complete Guide* in that its approach is more in depth. There are entire sections dedicated to Little League and high school football as well as insightful comments on coaching and parenting football players. Long's personal insights and sections devoted to conditioning and diet make this a top choice for young football players to read.

4. Tim Green's *The Dark Side of the Game* is a must read for the inside scoop on pro football. This book is interesting, filled with anecdotal stories both humorous and disturbing.

This list is by no means exhaustive. Any bookstore will have a complete section on football in the sports area.

In addition to reading up, be sure and go to the practices and games where you can observe theory in action.

So, there you have it. Now you should be ready to enjoy the game of football. As you can see, it is a technically complex game, but one that is filled with tons of excitement.

I hope this book has helped you in some way toward gaining a basic understanding of the game. Any comments you have will be appreciated. Just write or e-mail to one of the addresses listed in the front portion of the book.

# Here's wishing you happiness. And regardless of the score, don't forget to enjoy the game!

# GLOSSARY

**Blitz:** A defensive maneuver in which more than five defensive players rush the quarterback. The intent is to either "sack" the quarterback, or force him to make a quick pass. It is said that offensive linemen rush and linebackers blitz.

**Center:** An offensive position on the field. The center is the guy in the middle of the offensive line who hikes the ball to the quarterback.

**Conversion:** (Also called a two-point conversion) After a touchdown is scored, the scoring team can place the ball on the three yard line, then attempt to make another touchdown in one play. If successful, it is worth two points.

**Cornerbacks:** A defensive player located toward the back of the defensive alignment. His job is primarily to cover the receivers.

**Defense:** The guys who are trying to prevent the offense from gaining territory.

**Defensive Back:** A defensive player located in the backfield. Usually, cornerbacks, safeties.

**Defensive Lineman**:  A defensive player located just behind the line of scrimmage.  Usually ends and tackles.

**Defensive Tackle**:  A member of the defensive line.  There are two, lined up on the interior section of the defensive line.

**Delay of game**:  An infraction in which a player or team prevents the game from continuing normally.  The penalty is 5 yards.

**Down:**  Think of it as turns.  The offense has four downs in which to gain ten yards.

**End Zone**:  The ten yard area behind the goal line where touchdowns occur.

**Ends:**  A defensive player who lines up on the outside of the defensive line.

**Extra Point**:  The point after the touchdown where the kicker attempt kicks the ball between the uprights over the goal post.  It is worth 1 point.

**Face mask**:  An infraction where a player grabs the facemask of another player.  If intentional, it is considered a personal foul, and the penalty is 15 yards.  If unintentional, the penalty is 5 yards.

**False start**: An offensive infraction where an interior lineman moves after being set and before the snap. The penalty is 5 yards.

**Field Goal**: When the offense kicks the ball between the uprights and above the crossbar. It is worth 3 points.

**Flag:** The little yellow flag thrown by the officials during a football game when there has been an infraction or a rule broken. "There's a flag on the play" means a penalty is probably forthcoming.

**Flanker:** Also known as wide receiver. These are offensive players who usually line up on the side with the tight end just off the line of scrimmage.

**Formation:** The alignment that the offense or defense uses for different types of plays.

**Free Safety**: One of the two safeties on the defense. The free safety is lined up right down the middle of the field, in the back. He's literally the last line of defense.

**Fullbacks**: One of the offensive running backs. Usually leads the way for the half backs, but can run the ball and catch passes also. He's lined up in the offensive backfield.

**Fumble**: When an offensive player loses the ball by either dropping it or having it stripped during a tackle. The ball is then up for grabs by both teams.

**Goal Line**: The line located at each end of the field beyond which a touchdown is scored.

**Goal Post**: The post with a 'U' on the top of it at each end of the football field. The 'U' on top is called the uprights and the ball must go through this to score on field goal or extra point attempts.

**Guards**: The two offensive linemen lined up on each side of the center.

**Halfback**: One of the offensive running backs. He is usually responsible for carrying the ball on running plays.

**Hang time**: The time in which a ball "hangs" in the air after it has been punted.

**Illegal motion**: When an offensive player in the backfield goes into motion toward the line of scrimmage before the ball is snapped. The penalty is 5 yards.

**Illegal substitution**: When a player enters the field during the play. They can only substitute when the ball is dead.

**Incomplete pass**: A pass that is not caught by an eligible receiver or intercepted by a defensive player.

**Interception**: When a defensive player catches a pass intended for an offensive player.

**Kick returner**: The guy who runs the ball down the field after the kickoff.

**Kickoff**: When the kicker kicks the ball down the field to the opposing team. It happens at three different times during the game: The beginning, the start of the second half, and following any scoring play.

**Kickoff return team**: One of the special teams who receive the ball during kickoff.

**Kickoff team**: One of the special teams who kick the ball during kickoff.

**Line of Scrimmage**: The imaginary line on the football field, running parallel to the goal lines, (from sideline to sideline) where the ball is placed to start the next play.

**Line Stunts**: When two men on the defensive line exchange their attack positioning at the snap. It is a maneuver used to confuse and imbalance the offense.

**Man to man defense**: A type of defensive coverage in which each defensive player is assigned to a particular offensive player. See Zone defense.

**Offense**: The guys on the football field who are currently trying to get a touchdown or field goal.

**Offensive Linemen**: Those players on offense who are situated just behind the line of scrimmage. The offensive line consists of the center, the two guards, and two tackles.

**Offensive Tackles**: The guys on the offensive line located outside the guards.

**Officials:** The football policemen, judges, and juries. The spot infractions, interpret, apply and enforce the rules of the game.

**Onside kick**: A trick kick. During kickoff, it is the attempt by the kicking team to kick the ball just past the ten yards required, then recover the ball themselves.

**Penalties:** The punishment doled out by the officials for an infraction during the game. Penalties are predetermined, depending upon the circumstance.

**Personal foul:** A major infraction with a 15 yard penalty, a personal foul signal can be followed by a signal that indicates roughing the kicker, roughing the passer, or grabbing a face mask.

**Punt:** A type of kick where the kicker drops the ball and kicks it as it falls in an attempt to make it go as far as possible to the other end of the field. An offense usually punts on the fourth down.

**Punter:** The kicker that punts the ball.

**Receivers:** The guys on offense, also called wide receivers, who catch passes.

**Referee:** The official who is responsible for general oversight and control of the game.

**Returner:** During the kickoff, it is the guy who catches the ball and runs as far as he can down the field.

**Roughing the kicker:** A personal foul which occurs when a player hits the kicker's body or leg while he is in the act of kicking or if a player knocks the kicker down after he's kicked the ball. The penalty is 15 yards.

**Roughing the passer:** A personal foul in which a defensive player hits the quarterback after he has clearly released the ball. The penalty is 15 yards.

**Running Back:** An offensive player who usually runs the football. Running backs consist of fullbacks and halfbacks. They are located behind the linemen.

**Rush:** Two different definitions. 1.) Another term for a running play. 2.) A rush is also a defensive maneuver where the linemen literally "rush" at the quarterback in order to sack him or force him to throw the ball quickly.

**Sack:** When a quarterback is behind the line of scrimmage, attempting to deliver the ball and he is tackled.

**Safety:** Two different definitions. 1.) The defensive position on the field who is the "safety net" in the backfield. There are free safeties and strong safeties. 2.) A safety is also a situation in which an offense is tackled in their own end zone. The defensive team scores two points and the offense must now kick off from their own 20 yard line as though they had made a touchdown.

**Secondary:** Defensive players consisting of cornerbacks and safeties.

**Snap:** When the center hikes the ball.

**Split Ends:** An offensive player, also known as a wide receiver who lines up on the line of scrimmage on the side away from the tight end.

**Strong Safety:** A defensive player, one of the two safeties, who lines up opposite the tight end.

**Tight Ends:** An offensive player who acts as both a receiver and a blocker. He lines up next to the offensive tackle.

**Time out:** A rest period of sorts. The clock stops and won't start again until the ball is snapped. Teams are given three time outs per half, two each per overtime.

**Touchback:** Any time the ball is ruled dead on or behind a team's own goal line after it has been kicked by the opposing team, it is a touchback. Also, if the defense intercepts or recovers a fumble behind its own goal line and doesn't run it back into the playing field, it is a touchback. No points are scored on a touchback. But the benefiting team takes the ball on the 20 yard line.

**Touchdown:** The act of moving the ball down the field and across the opposing team's goal line is a touchdown. It is worth six points.

**Two point conversion:** After a touchdown is scored, the scoring team can place the ball on the three yard line, then attempt to make another touchdown in one play. If successful, it is worth two points.

**Unsportsmanlike conduct:** The use of abusive, threatening or insulting language or gestures to opponents or officials. The penalty is 15 yards, and if it is on the defense, it is an automatic first down

**Wide Receivers:** Offensive players whose job it is to catch passes. They line up closer to the sidelines than the rest of the team.

**Zone defense:** The type of defensive coverage where the defensive players defend areas or zones as opposed to man to man.

# INDEX

# COMING IN JULY, 2001 FROM
## JERSTEN PRESS

## THE BIG GAME

**A romantic fiction by: Helma Clark**

Drake Falconer is a burned out, former pro football star.
Samantha Sherrill is his number crunching business manager.
Join them as they lock horns and hearts in **THE BIG GAME.**

Turn to the next page for an excerpt ...

# CHAPTER 1

Drake Falconer stood beside third base like a huge sentinel, his thick black brows furrowed in disapproval. On the field- and it was a real stretch to call this Georgia wasteland a ball field- a group of fourteen year old boys moved about in animated confusion.

The Spenser boy was trying to pitch like Greg Maddux to the new kid, who apparently, had never hit a baseball in his life. Spenser's dad had paid a fortune for pitching lessons up north of Atlanta. He had described it to Drake as an investment in the future. David Spenser planned on retiring from selling real estate in six years so he could manage his son's pitching career.

As hard as Spenser was throwing the ball, Drake doubted the boy's arm would last through his sophomore year in high school.

The second baseman and shortstop stood nose-to-nose, ready to fight over field coverage. And the youngest Adams boy had lost focus ten minutes ago and was now chasing the center fielder with a dog turd hidden in his glove.

Drake watched the scene with growing frustration. He wanted to shout the whole group down, but there was so much noise in the background, he'd need a megaphone to be heard.

Some brain trust had decided to build new bleachers for this pitiful field two weeks before the season started. A swarm of men with hammers and power saws created havoc behind him.

The whole miserable situation, he thought, came eerily close to an analogy of his life-constant chaos and not one solid play.

It was enough to make a man head back to the NFL and destroy what was left of his knees.

"Looks like you've got help."

Drake redirected his attention to the one true friend he could claim. Grant "Flatus" Martin stood behind him like a big black advertisement for Green Giant Foods. He dwarfed Drake's six foot four, two hundred and thirty pound frame. And Drake had discovered in high school that the big guy's heart dwarfed his physical body.

"You?" Drake asked. "You hate baseball. 'A game for quiche eaters,' wasn't it?" he announced, repeating his friend's earlier statement.

"Still is. Not a drop of testosterone on that entire field. Look at that kid running from a little dog crap. If that boy was a real jock, he'd turn around and make Adams eat it, glove and all.

"Your boy's on short stop," Drake reminded him.

"His momma's idea."

Drake belted the titan on the head as though he still wore a helmet for a living. "You married well, Flatus. A woman with a brain... Who'd have thought you had it in you."

Grant rolled his shoulders in a way that was intended to remind Drake that he hated his nickname and despised the fact that the petite, soft-spoken woman he loved was a physician who tended to run the show at home.

"At least I wouldn't let a woman coach my team." He angled his head toward the new kid in the batter's box.

There, behind the backstop stood a young girl with the countenance of a momma lion. Grabbing the fence with both hands, she was apparently giving instruction to the new kid, which was obviously why the boy wasn't hitting the ball.

"Looks like Big Sis. She's telling him to back away from the plate." Drake knew he sounded offended, but he'd just spent twenty minutes on the novice, showing him exactly where to stand, how to swing the bat.

"Looks to me like she's backing him out of the box." There was laughter in Grant's voice.

Drake took a deep breath and tried to dismiss what was quickly becoming a throbbing headache. Four years of high school football, four years of college football, and four years of professional ball had yielded him two torn rotator cuffs, a fractured cervical vertebra, two torn medial collaterals, one ruptured meniscus, and an obliterated ACL. But no headaches...not one.

Now, for the last eight years, he'd had what everyone, including his ex-wife, considered a boring existence, and his life was literally filled with headaches, real, skull pounding, vomit inducing headaches.

"God save me from sisters," he muttered as he headed out of the fenced area and toward the backstop. Grant's laughter followed him the entire way, which made his head throb harder.

"May I help you?" His voice was sharper than he intended. After all, it hadn't been that many years ago that his own sister had stood toe-to-toe with a linebacker who'd knocked him unconscious on the football field. Diana Falconer had read the riot act to the three hundred pound college junior. She'd insisted that the mammoth apologize to her brother. And he'd done it.

The memory brought a smile to Drake. Even now, from more than three hundred miles away, his sister was still trying to protect him.

"Are you the coach?" The voice was filled with tension; actually, it sounded more like terror.

Drake nodded and tried for a softer tone. "My dad is the manager, but he's not here today. Can I help you?"

She pushed her coke bottle glasses up on a nose that was entirely too small to hold them and proceeded to inspect him thoroughly.

"I don't want him hurt," she stated flatly.

Drake was left speechless. The only woman who'd ever used that tone on him had been his mother, and only when Drake had messed up big time. It caused the hair on the back of his neck to stand at attention. A full ten seconds passed before he responded. "I'm sure you don't. And I can assure you that I don't want him hurt either. But if he doesn't stand up to the plate..." he motioned toward the white batter's box, "...inside that box, he can't hit the ball."

She continued to inspect him through her magnifying glasses. Drake was used to being observed by women. But this was different. Instead of the usual admiration, this girl's expression was analytical, as though he was some subhuman form and she was trying to recall the species. "Mr. Falconer-"

Ah, so she knew who he was. Some of the old confidence returned. "Drake. My dad is Mr. Falconer. And you are...?" He brought out the smile and handshake that usually sent women of all ages into stuttering fits.

The inspection continued, and Drake irrationally tried to recall what he'd had for lunch and if he'd wiped his face afterward.

Finally, she redirected her attention to the field and pointed an accusing finger at the Spenser boy. "You have a pitcher over there who is trying to prove...something. Now, I don't know much about sports. But it doesn't take more than a brain stem to figure out that a fourteen year old with a baseball in his hand and something to prove will eventually lead to...injury."

Charm hadn't worked, so Drake went for what this particular female obviously needed. Logic. "I admit, Spenser is a little aggressive. But his pitches aren't that wild. And at this level, it's rare for a boy to get hurt."

She remained unimpressed, her gaze pinned to the diamond where the catcher was trying to talk the kid into getting back in the box.

"If he gets hit-"

"That's what helmets are for," Drake assured her.

"But if he gets hit in the chest-"

"That's what ribs are for. The kid's got good reflexes; he just needs experience. He'll be fine."

She didn't respond.

Drake attempted a smile, but his patience was quickly disappearing.

The girl was a wreck. And he wasn't sure whether to treat her like an overprotective mother or sister. He'd learned after three years of coaching adolescent boys that the approach to each was different.

It was hard to judge her age. She didn't wear a speck of makeup. Her hair was a mousy brown and had probably never seen a stylist. But her body appeared to be filled out nicely under a nondescript tent dress. In Drake's educated opinion, she had potential, but didn't seem to care.

"Mr. Falconer."

"Drake."

That brought her assessing gaze back around. Drake was sorry he'd interrupted.

"Have you ever been hit with a baseball, Drake?"

Now this was comfortable territory. "I've been hit with a lot worse than baseballs. See that guy over there?" He pointed to Grant who was watching the interaction with great interest.

She raised an eyebrow and nodded.

"I've been hit by him at full speed." When she looked confused, Drake explained. "We played pro football together."

He'd expected an awesome, if not respectful response. In this world, women went nuts around the pros.

Obviously, she wasn't from this world. Her brows drew together into one grim line. "And you think that should make me trust you with my son?" He'd just been demoted from the subhuman category.

So she was the mother, a mother whose reaction to his former career was on level with one she'd reserve for a pedophile.

"Mrs...." Had she told him her name?

"Sherrill." Her voice was suddenly thin, almost a whisper. "And that boy's name, in case you're interested, is not 'kid.' He is my son, Andrew. He's never played baseball before. And the only reason he's here now is because I promised him I'd allow it if he'd agree to move here."

She squinted hard behind her glasses as though trying to search his soul. "Didn't they tell you about him?"

She was about to cry. God in heaven, she was about to cry. Drake's chest tightened. "They?" was all he could manage.

"Mr. Walker...the president of the youth league. He said he would explain."

Her composure seemed to be returning, so Drake asked the question that had been tickling his brain since the boy had shown up for practice. "Actually, no. And I was curious how he got on a team this long after sign-ups. Not that I'm not happy to have him. It's just that the cut off date was two months ago, and that's usually etched in stone-"

Her posture went from defeated to defensive. "Mr. Walker assured me that you wouldn't mind. If this is a problem-"

"No...No...It's just that...Sherrill. Did you say Sherrill?"

The woman nodded her head with a look of relief. "That's right. Your father-"

"Your husband-"

The frown returned with a vengeance. "My husband is dead."

"I see... I mean I'm sorry. It was just that, I thought-"

A loud, distressed whoop from the outfield provided a distraction. Drake's attention immediately landed on the Adams boy who had somehow tackled the big center fielder and was about to apply a fecal facial.

"Adams!" he bellowed, causing Mrs. Sherrill to jump. His patience snapped, he turned to her for less than a second and barked, "Sit! There!" He pointed toward the small bench where two other mothers were deep in conversation. "We'll discuss this later."

With his head splitting, he turned away from her toward a whole new piece of chaos.

**********

Samantha Sherrill glanced over at her son and was immediately met with a placating smile.

"You okay?" he asked.

"I'm sorry," she answered. Those seemed to be her favorite two words of late.

Andrew shrugged his shoulders in dismissal, and then turned his attention back toward the pitcher.

He was a good boy. More tolerant than any fourteen year old she'd come across. He was truly adaptable to just about anything. But then, he'd had to be.  It had been just the two of them for so long, just Andrew and his overprotective momma.

When Samantha came home two weeks ago with a bottle of sparkling grape juice and had told Andrew of her intention to move from their leaky old apartment in Tennessee to a nice, solid, state-of-the-art home in Hope, Georgia, Andrew had merely shook his head.

"Can't do it," he'd informed her.  "I've got friends."

Samantha's excitement had quickly dissipated.  While she had been spending the last fourteen years scraping and struggling for a way to get her son out of what she considered a hellhole, he'd been enjoying what he considered a happy life, one filled with, if not the athletics he craved, at least a good group of friends and a loving mom.  What more could a kid want?  Nope, he'd stay right here, thank you.

It was the first time since potty training that Andrew had dug in his heels and refused to budge.

Samantha-Sam to her friends-had never been one to give up a challenge.  And heaven knew she'd had bigger challenges than this one.  Hadn't she practically raised her son alone in the middle of the most gossip prone town in the US- A town where whispers of the Sherrill boy's parentage had been becoming louder of late?

Sam had proceeded to beg,˙ plead, and finally bribe her son into a better life.  Andrew hadn't wanted a bike or a skateboard.  He hadn't cared that in his new home he would have a huge bedroom, or that there would be a recreation room with a big screen TV. Playing with his friends was better than any TV. So Sam had swallowed every ounce of fear and trepidation and had bargained baseball in Hope.

Even in light of the euphoria she felt at finally being out of Tennessee and away from the past, she worried that it might all be a mistake. From the look of things, she was certain Andrew would be maimed within the hour.

She walked toward the bench to which she'd been relegated. New state, new town, new women to be shunned by. She was at what had to be the zenith of her life and things weren't looking good. For the first time in weeks, she worried about the future.

"You must be the new mom George told me about. " A blonde woman who looked like she'd just come off the cover of Vogue held out a perfectly manicured hand. "I'm Karen Walker... George's wife."

Her smile was big and sincere. Sam found herself reaching out in return. "You're Mr. Walker's wife?" The realization was a jolt. The president of the youth sports association was at least twenty years this woman's senior.

"Yes," she answered confidently. "Used to be his secretary. One of those. That's our son Ryan on first." She pointed toward a tall, lanky kid who had obviously given up on the whole mess and was sitting down on first base.

Sam was intrigued by the woman's candor. "I'm Samantha Sherrill. It's nice to meet you."

"We saw your moving van roll in just before practice. I'm surprised you're here."

"Our moving van?"

Karen smiled. "We live next door."

Sam thought of the huge stone Tudor next door to the house she and Andrew were moving into and felt her eyebrows rise in response. "Oh, my."

Both women laughed. The other woman with almost identical hair coloring, but whose features were sharper announced, "Karen likes a lot of space. And she has no manners. I'm Monica Adams. The hellion in left field is mine, although I hate to claim him."

She scooted over, allowing Sam to sit.

"I noticed him earlier." Sam tried to be diplomatic.

"Who didn't? Baylor tends to get attention wherever he goes. He's his daddy's boy. I've given up on taming him." She pronounced her son's name as "Bayyy-luh" in what Sam was quickly recognizing as the aristocratic Georgian accent.

During the three days she and Andrew had awaited the arrival of their moving van, they had stayed at a Holiday Inn just outside Hope. It was there, in the lobby of the hotel that Andrew had struck up numerous conversations and made note of the Georgian dialects.

"It's totally different from ours," he'd explained, as though Tennessee and Georgia were different continents instead of merely a state line away. He'd gone on to describe and emulate.

Sam was, as usual, amazed by what attracted Andrew's attention. Her mind usually wrapped around anything dealing with numbers. She rarely noticed more than the surface with people.

Andrew was a people person. He truly liked people and was interested in their individuality. While Sam had been holed up in her room at the Holiday Inn working over her new, healthy budget and studying potential long-term investments, Andrew had happily spent hours in the lobby of the hotel...talking. Like the Adams boy, he seemed to have taken on some of his father's characteristics.

Sam shivered.

Karen Walker interrupted her uncomfortable thoughts. "So George tells me you'll be working for Drake." She nodded toward the huge beast who was now making his way back from center field with his even bigger black cohort.

"Oh, no." Sam heard the abhorrence in her voice, and quickly tried to change tone. "I'll be partners with his father in the construction company."

The pair turned toward her like a couple of blonde Jack Russell terriers who'd just spotted a chipmunk.

"His father?" Karen asked incredulously. "Partners in Falconer Construction?"

Sam tried not to be offended. After all, it wasn't every day that a woman bought a partnership into a family construction company. Just because it had been a life-long dream for Sam to build houses didn't mean it was the same for all women. Not to mention the fact that it was rare for a single woman to have the funds to buy a partnership. She smiled at the excitement of it all.

"Yes. We came to terms two weeks ago. Diana Falconer is a friend of mine in Tennessee. When we...when I decided to move and start my own business, she suggested that her family was looking for a partner and business manager. She actually served as the intermediary for the deal."

Monica looked at Karen in blatant shock. "Does Drake know about this?"

Karen shrugged a slender shoulder. "I assume he does. He told George they were getting a partner when they were discussing the Haley project." She returned her attention to Sam. "Does he know who you are?"

It took Sam a moment to think about that. He seemed to have recognized the name, but then had mentioned her "husband." It didn't matter. She would be dealing with the father, who wanted to retire. According to Diana, her brother had little interest in the business aspect of the company and had agreed fully with the partnership.

"I don't think so," she answered finally. "But I won't be working with him anyway. John Falconer is my new partner. I doubt that I'll see his son unless it's at baseball games."

Both women's faces had suddenly become mysteriously blank. They looked straight ahead, directly at Drake Falconer.

Samantha Sherrill wasn't the people person her son was, but she wasn't totally insensitive to the environment around her. Something wasn't right. That, she was sure of.

For the second time that day, she worried about the future.

Look for:

## THE BIG GAME

## COMING IN JULY, 2001 FROM
### JERSTEN PRESS

ADVANCE COPIES AVAILABLE
JUNE, 2001

TURN TO THE NEXT PAGE FOR FOR ORDERING.

FOR ORDERING, CLIP OUT THE ORDER BLANK
BELOW AND MAIL TO:

JERSTEN PRESS
P.O. Box 688
McDonough, Georgia  30253-0688
***Please allow 4-6 weeks delivery for already
published items and 4-6 weeks from print run for
upcoming items.

---

Use this page for ordering .

☐    I'd like _____ copies of SNOT
BUBBLES! @ $8.95 per copy.

☐    I'd like an advance copy of  THE BIG
GAME @ $5.99 per copy.

Please include $2.50 per copy for postage
and handling

___ SNOT BUBBLES @ $8.95

___ THE BIG GAME @ $5.99

SUBTOTAL.................._____
S&H @ $2.50 per copy......._____

TOTAL ENCLOSED........._____

-----------------------Notes----------------------117

CROWD NOISE
DEAD BALL    FALSE START    HOLDING    ILLEGAL FORWARD PASS    OFFSIDES ENCROACHMENT

BALL HAS BEEN ILLEGALLY TOUCHED KICKED OR BATTED    PERSONAL FOUL    ILLEGAL USE OF HANDS    INTERFERENCE    ILLEGAL MOTION

DELAY OF GAME EXCESSIVE TIME OUTS    PASS JUGGLED IN BOUNDS & CAUGHT OUT OF BOUNDS    INTENTIONAL GROUNDING    INELIGIBLE RECEIVER    LOSS OF DOWN

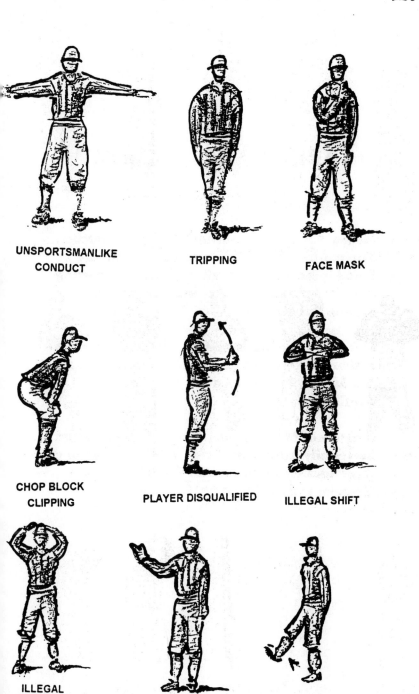

UNSPORTSMANLIKE
CONDUCT

TRIPPING

FACE MASK

CHOP BLOCK
CLIPPING

PLAYER DISQUALIFIED

ILLEGAL SHIFT

ILLEGAL
SUBSTITUTION

ROUGHING THE PASSER

ROUGHING THE KICKER

ANY MEN ON THE FIELD

# ABOUT THE AUTHOR

Helma Clark is a consummate game watcher. The mother of two active teenagers, she can be found year round at all manner of sporting events. "Watching the kids in action is a passion," she admits.

Her other passion is books. She is the diverse author of three novels and two plays. *Snot Bubbles!* is her first entrée into the world of nonfiction.

A native of McMinnville, Tennessee, Helma and her family currently divide their lives among three locales: Amelia Island, Florida; Macon, Georgia; and McDonough, Georgia.